Born With Voice

Nkwazi Nkuzi Mhango

Langaa Research & Publishing CIG
Mankon, Bamenda

Publisher:
Langaa RPCIG
Langaa Research & Publishing Common Initiative Group
P.O. Box 902 Mankon
Bamenda
North West Region
Cameroon
Langaagrp@gmail.com
www.langaa-rpcig.net

Distributed in and outside N. America by African Books Collective
orders@africanbookscollective.com
www.africanbookscollective.com

ISBN:9956-762-64-4

DISCLAIMER
All views expressed in this publication are those of the author and do
not necessarily reflect the views of Langaa RPCIG.

Acknowledgment

I won't forget my dear wife
Yes, Nesaa you're my wife
I'll always appreciate your contribution
You always keep me safe
Especially after long exhaustion
You always do good stuff
In our Altona language I say
You betcha or thank you

Our kids are our source of inspiration
We enjoy their admiration
Busy as I have always been
They always give us company
Nthethe (Kanthethe)
Ndidziwa (Ndiza)
Nthelezi (Nthe)
Ng'ani (Nyanyi)
Nkuzi (Kuji)
Nkwazi Jr (Genius or Prof)
These are our children
We are proud of having them

Prelude

Born with voice
Of course yes we're born with voice
Remember the time you're born
Never stop looking back now and then

We all were born with voices
Indeed, this is our reality
Truly, our voice is our reality
However sometimes our voices can be stolen

Voice your voices my friends
Or reclaim it when it is stolen
It is your own voice
Combine your voice with others'
Eliminate all injustices

I am not a snob
Neither am I a dodo
My voice is my source of power
Yes, with it I was born to win

The voice that all know
It has never had an alibi
It is with me day and night
My voice the weapon I came with

I don't like to sound like a spiv
Don't mistake this with braggadocio
Yet I am surely one of the literati
My voice makes me feel heroic
My voice is indeed my existence

This book is for victims
Yes, it is for victims
It is about the victims
It is about their fates and plights
It is for rape victims
It is theirs
Wherever they are
In whatever conditions they are in
In whatever countries they are found in
This book is theirs

This book is dedicated to the victims
Yes, victims of various vices
The victims of sexual discrimination
The victims of gender exploitation
The victims of cultural deterioration
Yes, this book is theirs
It is theirs wherever they are
In whatever conditions they are in
In whatever corners they are in
This book is theirs
It seeks to give them voices

This is the book of voice
Yes, the book seeks to create voices
Voices for the voiceless
Voice for all those whose voices
Were stolen
Those in silence
This book is unconditionally theirs

This book is my contribution
Yes, it is my contribution
Yes, the contribution to the plights of victims
Of whatever experiences and crimes
This book is a victim's book
Yes it a victim's nook

This book is but a prayer
It prays for cessation of causes of wars
It prays for the revolution in archaic cultures
Yes, the book is an eye-opener

The book is an ultimatum
Yes, an ultimatum to the world
It is but a world forum
It seeks to build the bond
It seeks to create a rostrum
The rostrum is the whole world
On which to address the conundrum
The victims have always faced

This book is a vexation
For others to come forth
Yes, it is an admonition
For others henceforth
To come and add on
Yes, we can't maintain silence
We can't keep in on with ignorance
While the victims are suffering

This book is about the voice
Yes, it is about everybody's voice
It seeks to rise up the voices

By making logical noises
It calls upon voices
Yes, voices of voices
To come and make the case
For various victims
The book raises the voices
It wants victims to be given voices
For they were born with their voices
So they need their voices back

Born with voice

I hear my voice
Yes, my voice
The voice I heard since
Since I came to existence
It has always maintains its presence
Yes, I hear my voice

We're all born with a voice
Sometimes we lose this voice
Some rob us of our voices
Yet, we need to have a voice
Voiceless need to have a voice

I'm here to invite every voice
Come voice your voice
It is about the voice
The voice against violence
My voice is the voice of peace
Yes it indeed is
It is a voice of justice

There's a belief in my culture
It is about the family that doesn't have a baby cry
It is regarded as a very sorrowful family
For babies bring blessings
When they raise their voices
They turn evil spirits away
They send them wobbly

When I was born I know
I was crying and kicking
Everybody does know
That when the baby's born is always crying
Announcing its noble coming
The same way I was born
The same way you were born
Everybody was born
We're born with our voices

Being born is not a new thing
Though, the one born is seen as a new being
Surely, for every individual is an in-thing
A unique kind of understanding
This how we come into being
It's unique moment to celebrate and treasure
The time when everyone becomes aware
That there is a new creature
Happy birth day to me
Yeah, it becomes a legacy of me
Yes, my voice is my legacy

Despite being a novice
Every creature comes with its voice
It introduces its voice
Yes, we hear its cries
The day it sees the radiance
The day it tastes annoyance
You'll hear this voice

Isn't the baby born with a voice?
What a sweet and unique voice!

All ears love this voice
The voice of sacredness
When the baby cries
Its voice makes melodies

Parents swell with joy
Neighbours come and enjoy
They say
"This baby is our joy"
The bad news however
As some grow bigger
They end up losing their voices!
Others maintain their voices
Others steal the voices of others

Though it is out of their choices
Many lose their voices
Some regain their voices
Others–forever–lose their voices
These are the ones
The ones that I speak on their behalf
One that can't speak for her/himself
He/she needs my voice
I'll always use my voice
To give the voiceless voices

So please lend me your voice
I want to add onto my voice
I want to offer this voice
To those that have no voice
For a human without voice
Is as good as dead

Everybody must have a living voice

I was born with my voice
With my voice to voice my annoyance
With my voice to show my happiness
With my voice to demand for assistance
Yes, I was born with my voice
All babies are born with their voices

I got my voice free
Why shouldn't I offer it for free?
My voice is free
It needs my free will
I want all to offer their voices for free
So that we can help the voiceless of the world

My voice is my weapon
It is the weapon to rely on
With my voice I'll soldier on
Making it heard here and beyond
Yes, my voice is my weapon
Your voice is your weapon

My voice is my weapon
Bombs can't silence it
Though they can imprison me
My voice won't have any of it
Always my voice is like a dissident
It will never be silenced
My voice will never be imprisoned
I won't be silenced
My voice will always rebel

My voice will make noises
It will disturb the oppressors
It will create rumpus
In the ears of my tormentors
It won't cower or surrender
It is always a winner
This is me
My voice is me

Life without a voice is void
It turned a person into a paranoid
A person becomes like an android
Such person is void
Like a shell he or she become void
A person should never live without a voice
Everybody deserves to have a voice

Life without a voice is a prison
Yes, a prison in oneself
It destroys oneself
One becomes like a serf
The person becomes like chaff
After seeds have been removed
Chaffs have no voice
But seeds have voices

Who wants such a miserable life?
Everybody deserves a meaningful life
Life without enriching oneself
Is as good as a lifeless leaf
Life must be lived fully
One has to own and enjoy it fully

Nobody can enjoy life without voice
So everybody must have a voice

Do you know what happen when a leaf dies?
It loses its greenish
It becomes peevish
Especially when the winds gush
It knows it has nothing to flourish
The person without a voice
Is like a fish in the desert
A person without a voice
Is like a lioness without a pride

Have you ever observed frogs in the ponds?
They make a lot of noises
What of birds in the trees?
They too make a lot of noises
They attest to their presence
They all declare their prominence
All creatures have voices

Sometimes beasts' voices sound meaningless
Yes, to us they are but pointless
Then they make meanings out of their voices
This is why they make such noises
We may perceive the voices of beasts as fuss
Yet they're not living in silence
Their voices have significance

Those who use silence as their voices
Are said to be but wise
If someone chooses silence by keeping the voice
That person has a voice
But when somebody chooses silence
Simply that person doesn't have voice
This is a crisis
We need to use our voices
To give that person a voice

Have your ever heard the voice of doves?
Yes, they use voice to attract lovers
At this time no dove cowers
They make their voices heard
They get what they need
If so what of us?
We need to use our voices

Our voices have a purpose
They're not useless
Neither are they meaningless
Our voices are our essence
Our voices are the purpose of our presence

So our voices are so important
We need to underscore that
With them we are smart
Without them we're but dormant

Money can't buy our voices
Wealth can't surpass our voices
With our voices we create things

With our voices we destroy things
It is only our voices
That put us above all beings
It is the only weapon
That we brought to this universe
Yes, we are born with our voices

You hear people go to the universe
What do they want to do there?
They want to plant our voices
Or make our voices heard
Whoever in the other part of universe
Must hear our voice

Our voices are the signatures
They make us different from other creatures
We have named all creatures
Just by using our voices
We sound and think with our voices
Yes, our voices of voices
Yes our inner voices

Our voices make us better
Because of them we're better
It will be even better and better
If we restore voices for others
Others who lost their voices
The others we see like mutters
As their voices fail to come forth

We need to use our voices
To voice whatever we want to put across
With our voice we are but soldiers
Yes, with our voices we get success
With our voices we are but heroes
Yes, with our voices we're heroines
We are truly champions
Of whatever we feel and want done
Whenever we raise our voices
We make and realize our choices

I was born with my voice
The creator gave me the voice
He or she hears my voice
Whenever I want responses
You too were born with your voice
So use this voice
Voice whatever you want to voice
Especially against injustices
Just raise your voice
Your voice can bring changes

My mother hears my voice
She knows it among many voices
My neighbours hear my voice
At nights and during the days
I send my voice
Yes I send it to the world

The world hears my voice
It understands my voice

How harder was it for my mom?
Having me when she's in a parental induction
Yet my mom soldiered on
With no regrets she carried on
She got used to, all of a sudden
To all chores and tribulations of having me

Though I was born innocent and cleaner
Yet I was branded a sinner,
I still wonder why calling me a sinner
How can an angel be a sinner?
Do those calling me sinner know the meaning?
Was I really a sinner?
Against whom did I sin?
How could I be while I was but a messenger?
A messenger of my own noble arrival
My voice refutes this
I was born clean and sinless

Didn't I cry when I was born?
Didn't I sneeze when I was born?
All these were the messages
Yes the announcements of my arrival
Yes, I screamed and cried surely
I made an announcement
That the angel has arrived

I was born harmless
I was born powerless
The only power I had was my voice
Yes it was my voice
That sent so powerful waves

The waves that caught everyone's thoughtfulness
Yes, I came with my voice

When the world heard my voice
Some say I cried because of joy
Some translated it in a different way
They say I cried because of sorrow
Some say I cried because of tremor
Everybody has something to say
It is either this way or that way
Again, I came with my voice

Despite my innocent arrival
They still condemned me
They right away designated me
Guess what they branded me
They branded me a sinner
They said I am naturally a sinner
I don't get it indeed
How'd I while I was dumbfounded

As I was still wondering
Yes, I was still studying
They added another allegory
They expanded the story
They said I was born a naturally a sinner
How can one be naturally a sinner?
A baby a reprobate!

Slowly I grew up
I found myself caught up
Caught up in their trap

11

The trap of branding me a malefactor
Am I really a sinner?
A person that needs pity
What for?

I believe I was born innocent
Yes I was born clean
Born without any taint
I was born unrestricted
Clean I was born
However, I was branded
Born free to question and doubt
Here I am posing the same request
Was I born a sinner?
Who decides who is a sinner?

I was born crying
I was born lamenting
Yes I was complaining
Whatever I tried to utter was vague
My vision was opaque
I was innocuously pleading
Asking for my mammy
I wanted to be nurtured
I wanted shelter
I wanted my teacher
My mother
My father
To explain why
Why branding me a sinner?
This is when I discovered my voice

The voice of rebellion

I was born with nothing except my voice
This is why I use my voice
I voice my anger and despondency
Yes, it is the only voice
That I came owning
Yes it is the voice I am using
It is the voice everybody must have

This is why I'll always cry
Through my voice I'll cry
Through my pen I'll cry
Always I will try
To make my voice heard
I'll speak for those unheard
I'll seek to have their voices heard
This is my noble duty
A sacred duty

I came with nothing except my voice
I will leave with just my voice
Even if I won't be able to use my voice
The day you will declare me lifeless
I will still use my voice
You still will use you voice
You'll describe me
You'll tell my story
Others will tell your story
They'll use their voices
To top up my voice

Without a voice you are as good as nonexistent
Animals have voices though they can't utter a word
Animals contribute in this world
They use their voices that are silent
Silence has the voice indeed
Through silence we can hear the sound
The sound of silence

I came with no money
I came without any pomp
Mine was but a yelp
I'll leave with no money
This is why I worship not money
How can I worship something illusionary?
Though I need money
I don't have to worship money
Yes I need money
I will never allow it to enslave me.

I came with my voice
I had no choice
Mine was to growl
As I announced my arrival
I invited all around to come and witness
The arrival of an angel
This is me
This is you
This is all

With my little legs I kicked
With my little fingers I grasped
With my little voice I cried

I announced my coming
Everybody heard me crying
My voice I was trying
To see if it is functioning

My voice was the only weapon I came with
I used my voice to get along with
All tribulations of life
When I feel unwell
I just did yell
My mom would wake up and take me
She would forget her sleep
She would have me to keep
She would swing me softly
Then I would sleep peacefully

My voice is the only wealth I came with
It is my voice that I have lived with
Wherever I am and whoever I am with
Everybody notices my presence
Just by hearing my voice
In joy and tribulations
It is only my voice
That links me with the world

I came asking for my mother
My consoler and protector
Yes my mother
The one that fed me
The one that brought me
The one that conceived me
She knows me

15

She knew me

She told me of her suffering
Yes, a nine-month suffering
Feeling dizzy and nauseated
Selecting food
Becoming picky and irritated
And many more tribulations
My mother strongly endured

She told me of her sleepless nights
Her half dead plights
Nine months of griefs
Nine month one leg in the world
And another in the vault

After I was born I became her master
I became her time keeper
My sleep was hers
Despite my bothers
My mom didn't criticize
With all heart and love she kept me
She saw me through
I strongly grew
Here I am
A much-respected man
Thank you so much my mom
You made me who I am

I had someone to lean on
Yes two important people to lean on
They stood by me in every situation

Everybody needs someone to lean
Even if he or she is a mature person
We still need someone to lean on
Despite having the voice
We still somebody to nurse the voice
We need somebody to nurture us
As we stand and use our voice

Do you remember your story?
I am sure you do remember
We all went through this trajectory
What a gift from our humble teacher!
Let me commemorate her
This is my tribute

Everybody has a story
The story that needs to be told
Yes, the story that needs to be heard
Life without a story is void
Such life is like a fishless pond
Nobody should live it
Everybody must tell a story
Our life is a story
Our voice is a story
So please tell this story

Go ask the mothers of the kings
Ask the mothers of the queens
Go ask their historians
Go interrogate their chroniclers
Did they come with their eminency?
Didn't they wear diapers?

They indeed did

However noble we may hold them
We may respect and fear them
Still they can't escape the realism
Didn't they come crying like all of us?
Didn't they come naked just like all of us?
Didn't they came helpless and defenceless
This truly shows
We all have voices
However we may be put in different classes
In the beginning and the end we're the same
We came with our voice
We'll leave with our voices

Go ask kings and queens
Will they go with their dominions?
Yes, when the time comes
The time of being tallied
Everybody will go empty handed
I know such reality is sad
Let truth be told
We're all vulnerable and weedy
Equality is our voice

We may deceive ourselves with this and that
We may as well offer all sorts of pretexts
Again the bitter truth always stands
We came with only our voices
We'll go back with our voices

Kings and queens came nude
Their servants too came naked
They'd nothing in their possessions
They only had their voices
They only had their desperateness
Just like any other creatures

Doesn't the chic cry when the egg is hatched?
I don't know of lizards
Again, I think they hiss
Their kings and queens too hiss
Hissing is crying just like human baby does

Do insects do the same?
I am sure they do the same
We can't hear their voices
We can't perceive their hisses
Yet they cry just the same
As human baby does

Even trees have voices
However we ignore their voices
Just because of our ignorance
They truly still have voices
Hear them when the wind blows
Intently listen to their leaves
They sing unique songs
They make life handsome

Listen to the trees when they are cut
Down they fall as they protest
They fall down crying and cursing

19

They weep with anger and twinges
You'll hear them groaning
They know it is wrong to have them cut

Nobody is truly born a queen
Nor one naturally born a king
It is out of human pomposity
That some are exulted
Other are belittled
It is out of their foist
That other are exploited
Again if we face the truth
Let's face the naked truth
Nobody is born above others

Nobody's born with any social burden
Nobody is naturally born a lumpen
Nor he or she with any crazy affiliation
Nobody is born a servant
Nobody is born a *bon vivant*
Nobody is born a master
We are all born equally innocent
We were all born litters
That is Mother Nature's edict
However we may deny it

Sometimes some beasts are better
I find goats dogs and camel to be better
They are born with the skin on their bodies
They are born with extraordinary abilities
So they are born with two things
They are born with their skins and voices

Aren't they better than us?
Who has ever studied this?

Donkeys, zebras and other beasts are smart
They are born naturally smart
With a moment of their nativity
They know their antagonists
They chew some pastures
They can run and camouflage

Insects are better than us
Aren't they if we face it?
Compare them with us
You will see another face
When a pupa leaves the nest
It doesn't need its mother
It starts to fend for itself
However facing tough life
It becomes the master of its fate
Aren't insects smart?

I saw my children being born
They all have one thing in common
They had their voices with them
I saw no differences
I saw no gendered preferences
Girls cried like boys
And boys cried like girls
They were all but babies
All equally born with their voices

Remember when your children were born
Weren't they as docile as anyone?
Hunger was their number one enemy
They'd grab whatever was handy
Sometimes they were happy
Sometimes they were grumpy
All babies are like that naturally
Again, they had their voices
Yes, they freely used their voices

They were born citizens of the world
Yet they found themselves confined
They were given narrow nationalities
Their high-end status was minimized
They ended up being labelled
They ceased to be what they used to be
They became subjects of policies
Good and bad policies
Ended up being given nationalities

Isn't this the prime sign of equality?
Our voice speaks with clarity
It starts from the outset
Soon the world will set in with it complexity
Silence will become a big punishment
One will be taught complicity
One will be taught about limits
Everything will have restraints
Slowly our voice will be affected
Some will be silenced
Some will be gendered
Our voice will be robbed

We need to have our voices

We will be taught about fear
Of course sheer fear
We'll be introduced to classes
We slowly will internalize such lessons
Slowly and methodically we'll end up being compliant
As we end up internalizing fear and it's aggregate

Born with our voices has its significance
Sometimes we'll become voiceless
Some of us will be divided
Others will be classified
Some will become noble
While other become ignoble
The story will however remain
Come shine come rain
We came with our voices

Try to ask yourself
Make a self-exploration based on self
Face it as you analyze it in its entirety
Are things truly the way we are taught
Are things so conservative and divisive as you see them
yourself?
Try to think by yourself
Come up with what you've discovered in yourself

Did the king know he was a king?
Did the queen know she was a queen?
Weren't they told by their mightier teachers?
Their mothers are their teachers

23

Their fathers are their trainers
We all have three teachers
We equally have three prime teachers
Ourselves, the world and our parents

However our parents are our teachers
They, too, have their teachers
They're students before becoming teachers
We, too, are students destined to be teachers
This is the nature of being a teacher
You need to learn before you teach
You need learn before you preach
For it helps us to explore our voices
We have our voice

I love my teachers
I respect my teachers
They shaped my adventures
They took time to shape my sphere
Without them I am nowhere
I will still be there however
Unnoticed, as ever

Who knows?
Who cares?
I'd have used my voice
To announce my existence
Again without their assistance
How would I have made it to prominence?
Yes, the one that every baby enjoys

My good teacher had no money
She had love and honey
She had milk and carefulness
She didn't demand any money
For whatever she did to me
She knew too well that I can't pay her with money
She knew money is but phoney
Don't be enslaved by wealth and money

If kings were not made to become kings
And queens to become queens
Do you think they'd become aristocracies
If servants were not robbed of their voices
Maybe they would have become kings
Or kings and queens without voices
They may have become servants
Well, this is the importance of the voice
Especially the voices of voices

My teacher was trustworthy
She taught me all that's compulsory
Given that she was also a prey
She didn't teach me dupery
She didn't teach me mockery
She taught me innocently and honestly

She did a lot of job
Teaching me how to gage
She had everything to describe
What a tough job!
What a noble job!

My mom taught me how to talk
She taught me how to walk
She gave me all tools of work
She didn't use any piece of chalk
Neither did she use any podium to talk
Her class was so meek
Wherever she could find time
She just taught me.

When I started crawling
My mom was there helping
She gave me all support
She said time and again
"My son stand up and soldier on"
Indeed. I did press on
Within no time, hurray, I crawled

Though it was a milestone
It had its repercussions
I started breaking things
Whatever that stood in front of me
Just became a fair game
I wanted to touch everything
My mom was there guarding

As I started to stand
My mother firmly stood
Yes, by me she stood
She provided motivation
I could hear her saying
"Go son go"
There I gave it a go!

"Go, go son go!"
My mother said

Slowly I stood by myself
I started walking as I wobbled
Starting walking was tough
All of the sudden, I was on my feet!
I started running
Not to mention falling
I used to come to her crying
After I landed on something

One day I tried to touch fire
My mom went haywire
It was a real quagmire!
It was for my mother an encounter
Of course, a tough encounter
Hers was to make sure I was secure
Learning was not a sinecure
It needed love and great care
My mom provided such care
She taught me to make sense of things!
She nursed my infant voice

The other day I grabbed a scorpion
My mother was shocked to the main
She thought that creature would harm me
Again, as fate may have it, it did not harm me
The other day I attempted to enter into a pit latrine
My mother rushed for me
She grabbed me
There I was once secure!

Yes my first teacher is my mummy
The one who taught me biology
She taught me how to hold her breast
I could hear the heartbeats of her heart
This taught me observation and curiosity
Then she taught me how to brush my teeth
She taught me math
When she sent me to the store
She went on teaching nutrition
She taught me relationship and ecological education
She indeed opened my horizons

She showed me my father
Without her how'd I have known my father?
She showed my neighbours
She introduced me to the doctor
She made me a communicator
She read my grim language
She patiently learned my language
Then she taught me her language
Their language

I still remember her lullaby
Indeed it was lovely
I wish I could go back to this spell
When everything for me was easy and well
I miss this time sometimes
However when I look at where I am now
Let bygone be bygone
I have to forge ahead
For, I have my own children
They demand the same from me

My mother listened to my lamentations
She bore with me as I displayed my peevishness
She consoled me when I was cantankerous
I remember how I used to sink my teeth in her body
She gently walked me through all such trying moments
What a selfless creature!

My teacher is the all-weather one
She is not a mere teacher
She is many things in one
My house for nine months
What a million-star inn!
She played all roles to make me happy
She became a musician composing sweet songs for me
She was my first settee
My first car and trailbike
My first medic
My first defender
Yes, my reliable protector

What a good storyteller who got me out of myself!
What comforter and caregiver
She forgot about herself
What a protector!
What a food taster who did not swallow before I did!
What medicine chewer who endured all bitter herbs!
I never heard her complaining
I never heard her cursing
Hers has always been protecting
Yes, caring
Sure, teaching
Teaching without end

I was born very lucky
I was born in the society
Where breastfeeding is the right
Where babies have their rights
Even if they can't pronounce them
For two years I enjoyed this right
I ate from my mother's chest
I ate and bit her teats
I ate till I said "I am satisfied"
As I grew up another teacher took over
My second teacher is the man
Yes the man who reprimanded me
The one who punished me
The one who initiated me
The one who told me to be a man
The one who inculcated his fear in me
The one who wanted me to be his reproduction
He owns me
I bear his name
I am his signature

This teacher was a hunter
A breadwinner
The teacher who feared failure
The teacher who always didn't sneer
The teacher who wants accomplishment
Yes dad is the teacher just like the mother
However he didn't change my diapers

This teacher was an adventurer
What a go-getter!
He pushed me beyond my power

He wanted me to succeed even more
To succeed more than he did
He wanted what he needed
In me his faith he restored
A no-nonsense sort of teacher
A teacher of a few words
My father borrowed some money for me
My parents denied themselves many things for me
They wanted to see me succeed
My success is the only thing they needed
It is because of their contribution
Yes, because of their devotion
I am here comfortably as I am
My parents made me who I am
They indeed nursed my voice
All children deserve this
All people deserve this
They need to have their voices heard
They need to have their needs attended

My first teachers taught me to be who I am
They taught me to be a parent
What I just do is but to repeat
Repeat all they'd in me to inculcate
They showed me the right
They nursed my voice
With which I make my case
They nursed the same voice
That nurses my children's voices

My parents sacrificed everything for me
Yet they knew I wouldn't pay them back

31

They knew too well I will pay to my children
Who will then pay to their children
It has been ever since the beginning

I was born in a very poor family
Again, for my parents' love and steadfastness
They saw me go through life successfully
Thanks to their selflessness
They took me to school
Thanks to their farsightedness
My life is cool
What else should I ask from them?
As said previously
There is no way I can repay them
Mine is to revere and respect them
They heard my voice
This is why I need everybody to have a voice

My parents told me clearly
They said it sincerely
They said they need nothing
Yes, they need nothing from me
They need only one thing
To fight for those who are suffering
To never forget where I came from
To never ignore problems people suffer from
This is their will to me
It always will be in me
Yes, I have to fight for the voices of others

I'll always venerate my teachers
I salute you my teachers

Everybody should do the same to those mighty teachers
Who made her or him what he or she is amid all wonders
I am a man today because of you
I have what it takes because of you
It is because of your well-done career
That I am here well

I can confidently stand with my hands akimbo
Yes, I stand and look back and mumble
With awe I am struck as I humble
Here I'm with full aplomb
Don't mistake me of a snob
I celebrate my parents' job
Yes, their well-done job
The job of making me

I thank my parents for promoting my voice
The voice that always everybody recognizes
Hadn't they had it to recognize
Who else would have it to recognize
They gave me all tools
With which to promote my voice
They skillfully had me guided
I was always in the safe hands

They gave me an education
That had my mind sharpen
They provided motivation
That inspired me to soldier on
With their knowledge and vision
I am who I am now

My third teacher is the world
What a very confusing world
Full of temptations and facades
Full of limitations and circumstances
Yes, the world is my educator
The world is my interlocutor
Whenever I uncounted new things
Everything has some strings

When the world starts teaching
You must obey its ruling
It creates all sorts of reasons
In almost all of its lessons
You don't reach any conclusion
Without following the rules
Sometimes you may break the rules
Yet there are values
Many things have ruses
Never abuse and never misuse
Teacher world will never pardon you
Neither shall it ignore you
It will severely punish you

Teacher world likes punctuality
So, too, teacher world likes self-restraint
Discipline is its most important tenet
Respect it and get it right
Mess with it and get its penalty
It wants everybody to become smart
It doesn't have time for regret

Sometimes the world is harsher
When you play out of its procedures
It can sometimes become a torturer
If you don't listen prudently
It can sometimes become a comforter
If you understand and obey the rules
So please use your voice to abide by the rules
You surely will live better

Teacher world has never lost
It is always a winner
Teacher world has no regret
Whatever it wants must be done
Whether you do or postpone
That teacher world has given
You'll one day do it
Whether you like it or not

My last teacher is myself
The one that the laws want to discipline
Whenever I break them
The one who stands all temptations
The one who braves illusions
Yes I am my last teacher and learner
Yes, it is me.

I am talking of myself
Me whom they branded a male
Yes me, the juvenile
Again, who told them that I am masculine?
Am not I something else?
They called my sister a female

35

Isn't she something else?
Anyway, she'll defend herself

As I grew up
My freedom was also caught up
Caught up in the trap
The trap of myths and disorders
The trap of commands and boundaries
I slowly adopted all such manmade rules
I am still looking for *womanmade* rules
I am looking for answers
Not for me alone
But also for others

My being teacher has its shortfalls
I will always be a student
Therefore you can see it evidently
I am a teacher-cum-student
There are matters I know well
There are matters I don't know at all
Everybody is like that
Nobody knows all

Despite having my voice
The voice I was born with
I still need to distinguish
Why I was branded a sinner
I need to get it right
So that the defence I can mount
I need to sort this out
I don't want to be a barrier
I have to move on

Without the banner of a sinner on me
Was I really born a sinner?
How while I was born a winner
Why sinners did call me a sinner?
Did they want me to be their helper?
In their confusion and conjecture
Again, am I truly a sinner?
Where did the winner me go?
Where did innocent me go?
Where did innocent you go?

Now that I am mature
I say I am not a sinner
I was born a winner
I was born cleaner
Than those who branded me a sinner
Never shall I be a sinner
I won't accept the title of the sinner
They must hear my voice of resistance
They must understand my line of sensibleness

Some said I did surrender my voice
Never shall I surrender my voice
They spoke on my behalf without my approval
They brought their God and views
They branded one of theirs
While I was not of theirs
I am myself
Born free and a winner
Born sinless

They said whatever they said
Did they know who am I?
Being with them for long
They have always got me wrong
They have nary understood who I am
They keep on guessing
When I was born
They said, "He's been born"
When I die
They will surely say he's died
Can I die?
Please don't kill me
For I don't die

How say you I die while you don't know me?
When you say I am dead
Ironically, you just bury my body
You divide my estate
You then forget me
You can't bury me
How can you bury me?
While you have never known me

Let me teach you a lesson
You who pretend to own wisdom
Stop pretending you know me
Do you know yourselves?
Where is your wisdom?
The one you used to intimidate me
The wisdom that branded me
The wisdom that unfairly judged me
Do you know me?

If you know me
Why do you bury my body but not me?
If you really know me
Why do you pray for my soul but not me?
Yes, I am me
Me the one that doesn't die as you reason
You'll bury all that belong to me but not my voice
My voice is eternal
It will live after my body is gone
My voice is like soil
You can't bend it with words

I don't buy into your ignorance
Your fanaticism
Your chauvinism
Your -isms of victimization
I am an independent one
The one that you have nary unwritten
Yes I have a voice

I am in my opinion
Unique as I remain
Self-aware than anyone can declaim
Yes I am myself
I know myself
I am not a criminal
I am not what you call me
I am who I say I am
Hear my voice

Some people pretend to love me
How can you love me?

Love yourself first
How can you love me?
If I die you get rid of me
You put me in a grave
Why don't you come with me?
Forgive me
I don't want you to follow me
For everybody has her or his own day.

Again, the question remains
Who am I?
Am I what people wrongly think or more than that?
Am I a mystery that nobody can decode or what?
Indeed, I am
My voice tells who I am

I was born an innocent being
I was born a sinless being
This is my nature
I need no concoctions and conjecture
I can say this for sure
There is no natural sin
This doesn't need any din

I was born without teeth
Yet somebody lent me her teeth
When I get old they will go
I was born without stable feet
My mom offered me a lift
As I age, my feet will go
I was born without connections
Then my family established ones

Her now I am
Why don't I thank them?
I am like a meteorite
I am not here to visit
I have the mission to convey
Like a meteorite fires through the sky
I too will shoot up and vanish in the oblivion
I will go where I used to be before being born
This is why mundane things will never intimidate me
My voice informs me
That I am more what you think I am

My friends and enemies believe me
Death will nary liquidate me
Though people will say it has taken me
It won't intimidate me
For it won't finish me
I will still live thereafter
Everybody will talk about me
I will live forever

Writing such words
It is but my signature
Are forever my words
Scripta manent
What is written is forever
My voice is forever
Yours too is forever
We're forever
Fear nothing though
Stand and make your voice heard

Yes, my voice is forever
It'll be heard forever
I thus have to write and holler
To speak for those who can't
This is my duty
My duty is to give the voice
Yes, my sacred duty is to give voices
Life is about voices
The voiceless are as good as lifeless

Victims of rape

I'm introducing a mother
I am presenting a sister
This is none other than a victim of rape
Yes, the victim of rape
The one who gives a yelp
Whenever she remembers what she went through
Her life's become a hoosegow
She is nothing but a loner
Sorrow is only left of her
She is the shade of herself
She lives with grief
Everything for her is tough

What this victims knows are insults
Yes, she goes through many difficulties
She's become an outcast
After being raped
Everything has crushed
She needs our support
She needs our hand
Let's give her the voice

Wherever she goes she's received by innuendoes
Her life has become nothing but scandals
Her life and that of her baby have become *candles*
They are burning in their own purgatories
They need to get back their voices
Yes, they need to be given back their voices

The victim of rape is called a whore
Yes, a hookery whore
Is she truly a whore?
Did she consent to being violated?
Abusing such victim is absurd
We need to put it to an end
How can we become a blind world?
A brutal world
A victimizing world!
Yes, we seem not to be moved
While victims are suffering
What are our voices for?
If we can't protect victims
Aren't we accomplices

This is the mother without voice
Yes, a voiceless sister of ours
Yes she is our sister
She is our mother
She is our aunt
She is our kin
She still is a woman

Despite living in miseries
Suffering from grief and horrors
She still is human like us
She courageously carries her distresses
Still she deservedly is human
Yes, she naturally still is a woman
So please treat her like any other woman
A woman of substance
Yes, a woman with chastity

Avoid branding her a sinner
Don't regard her as a loser
No, she must have a chance
She has a voice
Give her this voice

She is a woman like other women
She needs loves just like everyone
Yes like every woman
She needs care and protection just like any human
She breathes and suffers like everyone
She is one of us
She is a woman
Yes she's human
She is a human
However she's robbed of her voice
She still deserves human rights
Afford her the voice
She will fight for her rights

Let me tell you how it started
It started with greed
Some hyena-like politicians wanted power
They conspired to grab the reins of power
They said come shine come rain
Power must be ours
They didn't care about the consequences
They didn't care about others
Theirs has always been influence
Even if it means by killing others
This is how they killed others
This is how they displaced others

This is how they raped our sisters
Yes, they raped our mothers

They started their brutal wars
After they acquired weapons
Yes, western countries supplied them with weapons
Billions of dollars exchanged hands
Have you forgotten blood diamonds?
Criminals ganged up in the bushes
They fought their venal governments
They turned their countries into ruins
They did it hopelessly
They fought mercilessly
Many victims they produced

Some people were killed
Others were maimed
Many were displaced
Above all, women were raped
Girls were raped
Children were molested
Again, in the end
They created an unending trend
The trend of violence
The vicious circle of violence

The trend became a tragedy
For it has become universal now
Victims still live in sorrow
Displaced as they are
Shunned as they are
Many have suffered

After finding rape was effective
They baptized a "weapon of war"
Is rape really a weapon of war?
To me, rape isn't a weapon however
It is a criminal behaviour
That needs to be stopped
All behind this stupidity
Need to be behind bar forever

When war broke out
This victims lost security
Wondering in the hideout
She ended up being raped
She had her chastity robbed
Here she is facing all sorts of disgrace
She has lost her voice

Other were raped in their homes
When their houses were invaded
Rapists broke into their homes
With cruelty rapists pounced
They violated women
They violated girls
They robbed them of their voices

Let's go back to this woman
After her life became a ruin
Everyone threw a scorn
The victim was looked down
She became a second-class citizen
She was no longer valued
She was no longer accepted

For, she lost her voice
She has lost her face
She has lost her chance
Stigma is what she faces

The effects of rape are horribly deeper
They reduce a person into a ruin
The consequences are so deeper
In the victim's heart and brain
Understanding them is not easier
They create deadliest pains
That the victim suffers
We need to understand
So that we can help

Women have much understanding of the crime
They deeply know the effects of this crime
For, they know the real value of being a woman
Though it can be a bit hard for men
Shall they will, they'll understand
Men's understanding is shallower than that of women
I think it is only raped men who can understand this
phenomenon
When I step in victims' shoes at least I get a meaning
It is so confusing
Imagining is a to-do
What we need to do
Is but help the victims of rape

A rape victim suffers a lot
Rape leaves nothing back but torment
It creates anger and regret
Those rot and ferment
They flood the heart
They attack the brain
Then comes a perpetual pain
That's not easy to explain

Some call her a whore
They forget she's the mother
How would you feel?
If your mother is called a whore
How'll you reply?
If your mom is called a whore
Why don't people understand a simple fact?
That the victim didn't author her plight
What a poor creature!
Who wants to become a loser?
She verily needs our assistance
They long for our indulgence
Let give back their voice

She's nobody to call hubby
This victim won't have a hubby
The one who violated her is but a flabby
He is but a criminal
He is but namby-pamby
When it comes to manhood
Such a creature is but a ninny
That deserves to die in the quod
Even though he deserves a voice

49

Stealing others' voice
Denies him of his voice

Her dreams were shattered
Her future was ruined
She'll never be respected
If she is blessed
She'll regain her life
Yet the scars will never go away
Hers is a silent soliloquy
It is only through restoring her voice
The victim can have a place
Yes, it is through giving back her voice
That's when she can live in peace

A victim of rape is like an empty sack
An empty sack cannot sit upright
She is like an empty hammock
Yes, the empty hammock can't swing
Without anything put in it
Swinging needs weight
Like the hammock and sack
The victims needs something
That something is comfort
With care and comfort
They'll be able to stand upright
With love and support
They'll overcome all adversities

The rape victim needs to be refilled
Her full-of-honey pot is empty
If there is anything

It is nothing but dirt
If there is anything, it is nothing but regret
For those whose pots were not broken
Those who got some sutures
Mended were their bodies
Their souls are still broken
They are but browbeaten
They need only one token
Giving their voices back

Victims of rape are like a broken harp
Can it really have someone to harp?
Like a broken cup
Many would like to flatten
Others would like to scorn
Before doing all such mockery
Ask yourself sincerely
What I'd do if it were me
How would I like to be treated?
Of course, the answer is clear
Only the important thing I would need
To have my voice restored

When one woman is violated
The whole society is violated
We need to make her pains ours
Her voices lost is our loss
To help such a victim
Is but to help the whole society

I sincerely hate rapists
To me they're like contagious insects
I have no atonement
When it comes to hating rapists
These creatures are beasts
Even though they've human facets

A rapist stinks like a rotten fish
Recollecting his acts makes a victim feverish
She wishes he may abruptly perish
Maybe such punishment can reduce her anguish
Yes, such a person is but rubbish
Rubbish of manhood
He is but a dodo
Though he mighty walk around with bravado
Such a person is but a mere dodo
Rapist isn't a man but a yo-yo
That deserves to be treated with to-do

Rapists are like houseflies
You know what houseflies are good at
They contaminate clean nutrients
They fill everything with filth and diseases
They land on faeces
Then they jump and land on our dishes
Quickly they spread diseases
All diseases have remedies
The remedy of rape is life sentence
Life sentence without conditional release
Life sentence without clemency

A rapist is like a venomous snake
The snake with poison that's uneasy to dilute
It leaves victims morally and socially destitute
Forever cursed is this spineless snake
His effects live for ever and ever
He leaves his victims affected forever
He destroys life forever
So he doesn't deserve any honour
His is confine him in the solitude

Some regard the victim as a useless person and a loser
They don't want to get even closer to her
When she needs a helper
They just shun her
She becomes untouchable
To them she is but damage
The day she was brutally violated
She became easily reproachable
The day she was robbed
She became unwanted

Why our society is behaving this way
What a strange way
To behave
It seems we are carried away
Yes, ignorance has carried us away
Such a way, by the way, has logic to defy
Treating victims like a housefly
Is but debauchery
Who like a housefly?
The victim of rape is a prey
We need to restore her vanity

Shunning her we become predatory

I know her name
Though I won't name her
Privacy is important for her
Just as it is for any other
I know she used to enjoy fame
Before rape destroyed her
Now she faces the shame
Long gone is her future
Long gone is her stature

She's bitten by poisonous vipers
Yes human adders
Such bad creatures
They left their poison in the victims
Then they abandoned the victims
Ironically such devils are called men
What type are such men?
Are they men or just bad omens?
Such beings are but morons
They are not humans
They're but mere ramp-fed ronyons

A true man does not commit rape
A true man is a protector
A man who commits rape
He is inferior than ape
He should be castigated
He should be castrated
He should have his *balls* crushed
He'd never be given any remedy

A true man respects others
A real man doesn't violate others
A man who destroys others
He'd not be treated like a human
How can he be treated like human?
While what he does is inhuman?
Humans are human because of their humanity
Once they embark on inhumanity
Their humanity ceases to have weight

I abhor rapists
They are but dirty beasts
However they've human aspects
They still are noxious beasts
Beasts that should be quarantined
Beasts that'd die while imprisoned

Rapists don't deserve any pity
How while what they do is totally dirty
Theirs should be in the pit
Where there is no light
They'd be kept in a deep extremity
In order to contain their criminality

A man who doesn't contain his sexuality
He is as good as a rat
Even the rat is better
For it was created a beast
A man should not act as a beast
Otherwise he is but a beast

I weep for our mothers
My consolation is to my sisters
I can see how they suffer
Yes, the victims of rape
I honour such mothers
Mothers living with angst and pains
Women whose honour went to the drains
Just because some beasts raped them
I pray they recapture their voice

I wish the world should change
Let's embark on change
Let's give raped mothers another chance
So that they can live in prosperity and peace
Let's seriously detest violence
Yes, rape is violence
It silences the victims
It robs them of their voice

I know this is sinister
It is a scandal to utter
Yet it is true
This mother is a victim
This is true
She ended up conceiving a baby
Just after being raped
The baby without voice
The baby without choice
The baby who's robbed of its voice

She's born with her voice
Now she maintains silence
Rape robbed her of her voice
She needs our voice
To truly make her case
We need her to redress
To make sure she wins
She gets her voice back

Despite all such fears and worries
Fears of trauma and all sorts of disgrace
This mother soldiered on
She decided to bear all pains
To carry the baby for nine months

When her baby's born
It was called a bastard
Who actually is a bastard?
Is it the baby or those who had its mother raped?
Is it right to demonize such a baby
Is it fair to traumatize such a baby?
The best thing's give this baby its voice

Everybody's the mother and baby to scorn
The baby becomes its mother's badge
It becomes a badge of shame and disdain
Again, did such mother wish to be raped?
Why don't we want to understand a simple thing like this?
Aren't we the part of this brutal conspiracy?
Is this what is required of us?
Again, if we need solace
We must restore the voices of the victims

I see many children
They are facing a lot of suffering
Being born fatherless
Being born helpless
They need our supports
We need to give them voices
We must find their voices
And make sure that they're resumed
Yes, we need to offer our hand

Such children need an education
They're just like any other children
Who will pay for their tuition?
Who'll provide inspiration?
They need somebody to lean on
In this world full of indignation
Let's make such children move on

Such children need fathers to go to
But there are none to go to
Their identity becomes incognito
This should not be tolerated
Such children should be protected
The society needs to provide protection

This challenge is ours
We do not have any excuse
We must imagine if it were us
Or those dear to us
This way we'll realize
That is better for us to practice
If we step into their shoes

We'll know how to help them

Victims of rape are the voiceless
They need our voice
They have lost their space
They too have lost their voices
Our voices should be theirs
At least to see them through
I thus call upon everybody
Please come everybody
Join me in this attempt
The attempt of redressing rape victims

The lives of victims are tough
Whatever they go through is rough
They verily need our support though
Let's be their refuge
Let's fight this diabolic umbrage
Let's make our voice a suffrage
We need to stand with courage
To stand with the victims of rape
Let's give them hope

I can see a woman
Yes, I see a woman
She is like any other woman
However the difference is that
She's the victim of rape
And she has lost hope
You can't know her by her outward look
However, she has a big burden in her nook
She's morally in bad shape

59

Like razor, her pains are sharp
Like a broken harp
She has lost the voice
She needs her voice
We are her voice
If we truly give her the chance
She may get her voice back

She's looking for our support
Yes, she verily deserves it
Let us fulfil our duty
Why can't we take on her assailants?
I can see even some perpetrators
They are called warlords
They are in various capitals attending conferences
They pretend that they are looking for peace
Peace without redressing rape victim
Peace for whom?

I want to tell politicians
Those who use violence as their only means
The means for grabbing power
The means to evil prominence
What they are doing is an offence
It is a mass violation of women
Such politicians are quacks
They are but political junks
True politicians use votes
Yes, they use democracy
Democracy is the surest way to get to power
Democrats respect people power
They bank on policies but not on guns

Stop this lunacy

Power by violence is slavery
Power by rape is treachery
True power must be obtained truly
Truly through playing by rules
I want to tell warmongers
And their masters
You're destroying our sphere
Your greed is but papery
Soon you'll pay dearly

Go ask Charles Taylor of Liberia
Ask even Laurent Gbagbo Ivory Coast
They banked on their mania
However, it came with a cost
They are now in a crucible
Their voices are now inaudible
And their victims are inconsolable
They thought they are irreproachable
Where are they now my dear?

If Angolan Savimbi were alive
He'd tell his painful narrative
He thought he was indestructible
While he was but a perishable
He died like dog
His body's displayed like that of the hog
For all eyes to despise and abhor
He is rotting in a hole
What else for such a bore
Let's support this victim of rape

She's really in bad shape
We are her only hope
When she decides to talk
Let's listen to her little talk
Venting what she went
Through
Yes, what she went through
When she talks don't laugh
Just give her the support
Let's create space for such victims
Let's stand by them with no whims
Aiming at seeing them through
Through this censure
Let's stop this culture
The culture of silence in rape victims

We need to hear their stories
Let's give them chance to tell their stories
We, too, must lend them ears
So that we can hear their narratives
We need to respect their feelings
So, too, we need to respect their privacies
As we let them vent and move ahead

Let's step in their shoes
We need to feel their woes
We must to stop their throes
Let's condemn and stop wars
Let's share their burdens
As we fight to have them redressed
We must struggle to have them rehabilitated
So that they can move on

This woman will always go head down
Her child too will be downtrodden
Living such shameful life
Is in itself strife
We need to console them
We need to rebuild them
Let's give them some sympathy
Let's show them empathy
For they are human as we are

I wonder
When I see this world
People are good at judging
They, too, are easy at forgetting
Instead of abusing this mother
Why can't we bother?
At least to find the answer
We need to find this answer
The answer is to give them voices

We need to find solutions
After asking important questions
Who started the wars?
That made this mom a victim
Who supported these wars?
That caused mayhem
Please try to think
Please stop judging the victims
Instead give them their voices back
For they need them back
We know warlords started many wars
Yes, they have caused a lot of scars

To their people and their countries
Again, were they alone in these barbarities?
No, they had other accessories
Those who supplied them with weapons
Those who bought illegally obtained resources
All those should be brought to book
Yes, they must not be let off the hook

Warlords are criminals
Those conspiring with them, too, are criminals
Those supplying them with weapons are criminals
They deserve to die behind bars
The world must stop pampering criminals
Yes, some are pampered under pretexts of negotiations
Criminal should be posted to The Hague
Doing so will give voices to the victims

I see wars everywhere
War in Somalia
War in Mali
War in Nigeria
War in the DRC
War in the CAR
There is war in South Sudan
I see the victims of rape
Victims without voices

I see victims of rape in Darfur
Yes, there are a lot in the DRC
I see them in Nigeria
Yes I see others in Somalia
They are all over the place

Where violence is
They are almost everywhere
In war zones
In our streets
In our homes
In our schools
Yes I see them everywhere
As they face the quagmire
Their lives are dire
They need their voices

Rape victims are women
They're just like any other women
They need to be respected as women
Their womanhood is their token
It brings perfection
Violating their womanhood is a sin
Yes, it is a crime
It is as sacrilegious as any menace
Let's respect womanhood
By having it redressed
Through providing a voice

Rape victims are the children
All those born out of this ruin
They'll forever suffer indignation
If we don't turn the wave of their pain
Let's nurse their wounds
Let's have them redressed
Let's have them supported
We need to care about them
So, too, to care for them

We need to sympathize with them
By giving them the voices

They need our understanding
They badly need a good standing
It is through our good doing
Such victims may've peace
It is through our commitment
Such victims can recuperate
It is through our support
Such victims can regain trust
Otherwise they are given their voices

Let's bring together our voices
The voices of justice
Voices for justice
As we condemn injustices
It is through our adherence
Victims can get some solace
This does not need monies
It only asks for our voices
That'll give them their own voices

Rape victims need love and care
But not despair
They need someone to care
Someone they know listens
Someone they know recognizes
Their feelings and their splendours
That someone gives them voices
Those robbing them this gift
They must be made to appreciate

That what they're doing is corrupt
No woman should be treated this way
We must have criminal confined
Far, far away from humanity
Let's raise our voices

We say we're civilized
How if we are wicked
Civilization is humanity
Why then treat women with deceit
Why then treat women cold-heartedly
Rape is a crime
That everybody must combat
Let's raise our voices

I see women sobbing
They are dying
Silently they are dying
They are dying of the infamy
The shame of being raped
Rape robbed them their voices
For they were left with no place
They're but outcasts in their societies

Despite all insults
This mom didn't look back
She decided to fight good fights
She kept the baby in her cavity
Her kid is a permanent reminder
Of what she went through
Seeing him or her
Makes her suffer

It is a life of sweet and bitter
Memories of brutal life
Life with lost meaning
The life of suffering
Voice will give it the meaning

Nine months thereafter
Here the baby is born
This victim still had a lot to suffer
Whose son many would question
Her answer will be but humiliation
Her heart will be broken
Her face will be hidden
But again,
She is a victim who has no voice
What she needs is voice

This is the beginning
For many will repeat the same thing
They'll always put the victims on the cross
As if this was their choice
Their presence will become annoyance
Where will they put such *abeyance*?
Ours must be to stand by them
To care for them
Listen to them
Above all accept them
As we restore their voices

This mother will be a victim forever
We can stop this haunting process however

We can reduce the pangs of her encounter
We can redress her
Even the child born of her
They'll all face the horror
They'll go through shudders
Caused by horror of being born without a father
Caused by being a fatherless child's mother
Caused by lack of having voices

Seeing her begging in the streets
Seeing her being shunned from her communities
It must alert and disturb us
So that we can do what is required of us
Let's be courageous
To stand and say at the top of our lungs
Let's say enough is enough
Let's be a little bit tough
We must stop rape by all means
This will give females their voices

When you look at a child born of the victim of rape
You see the same thing with a gape
Victims of rape are in a trap
They verily need our help
Let's seriously have the heart
Let's question our heart of hearts
Let's penetrate victims' hearts
Maybe we'll see the light
We'll see what their hearts emanate
Then we'll find their voices
And give them these voices
The child will lean on one pillar

Mother is the only available pillar
Another pillar will be amiss
And its effects will have hardship to cause
It will kick in and become a torture
Especially in archaic culture
Where single motherhood is seen as an error
This is the plight of a child and the mother
They'll live anonymous
For they lost their voices

The child will always ask the mother
"Where is my father?"
Then the mother will remember
She'll recall all the horrors
Silence and aguish will veil her
She'll have no word to utter
But only to let out her tear
That'll provide no answer
Silence
Sobs
Weeps
There is no voice

You can't call such a child an orphan
It even hard to explain
What its mother went through
Every attempt becomes tough
But we still need to find a way
Through which to address this conundrum
It is a hard process to go through
Yet we need to address it though
It is only through giving them the voices

The child will want to know
If it is not today it is tomorrow
Knowing is a kid's right
Even if it will end up in torment
We need to let the child know
If in case he or she wants to know
Here is where the mother is tormented
Here is where we need to show we're concerned
Truth will give the child a voice

Asking the whereabouts of its father
The child will have the mother to torture
The mother will cry and holler
Sometimes she'll turn her anger at her youngster
In the end she will murmur
"Lord, why me and this horror?"
The mother will live in fear
Fear of what she encountered
The fear of her own child
The fear of her own past
She will become an outcast
Stonewalled she will become
She has lost her voice

It'll take long for a kid to understand
It'll be harder for the child to withstand
The child will experience a different world
What a torturous and humiliating world!
The child will grow disheartened
Everything will be perceived with a doubt
Due to having no voice

This mom didn't choose this end
To have her value robbed
To have her child illegally sired
This victim of rape didn't choose
She didn't make any lapse
To have this burden on her head
It is because of manmade rust
That we need to fight the hardest
Making sure she gets a voice

We need to educate our communities
So that they can become repositories
So that they can became refuges
For the victims and their relatives
They need to change their behaviours
Towards the fatalities
Re-victimizing victims makes it worse
We need to give the victims the voice

Shunning them is next to a crime
Traumatizing them is but ignominy
Why does a society bully?
Is it because of folly?
Some wrongly think that is candour
Again, the victims need a help
They need upkeep
For they're not the author of their predicaments
They didn't choose their torments

Some go for drugs
Others go for vengeance
Some attempt suicide

Yet they get no remedy
They end up suffering even more
For once problem causes another
They truly need our hand
To give them voice

Some victims flee their homes
They go to big rookeries
Some end up in *hookeries*
They run with rookies
For fear of rapists
For their rapists happened to be men
They see no difference in men
For some of them robbed them of their voices

Some victims end up hating every man
To them every man becomes a rapist
They generalize their angst
Such a trend leaves them torn
Between what is really and what is not
It becomes so difficult
For victims to judge with impartiality
If some men could take on this criminality
Maybe victims may see the light
And go back to their normal life
Yes, they go back with their voices

Some victims face it
They stand their ground
They don't allow victimhood to torture them more
They come forward and declare
Some offer forgiveness

They pick themselves up and press on
They nurse their wounds
As they seek their voices

Some become born again
They try once again
They embrace religion
Then soldier on
These are the winners
Whose voices they reclaimed
Yet despite all such courage
They still need our hand
Let's give them voices

Some wish a lightning could descend from the sky
To come and seal their fate
They wish everything could come to an end

Theirs always is why?
"Why us?"
Theirs has always been why
Yes, why without an end
"Why to us should this happen?"
With anger and a great pain
However, why'll never go away
Otherwise we decide to standby
Yes, if we stand by their side
They can regain their voice
Their hearts are broken
Their souls are downtrodden
Their humanity has been stolen

They live in the state of denials
For they are treated like anti-socials
As they ask why, why
Without knowing what to do
They're left in a limbo
We need to give them voices

Their fate has become a story
What a bad story!
It is a story full of sorrow
For such victims without tomorrow
The victims made immoral
We need to redress these sufferers
So that we can create a bright tomorrow
This tomorrow won't be practical
Shall we not give them voices

I see them in the streets
Yes in many streets
I seem them begging
For they've nobody for them to care
They have a lot to bear
Fending for their youngsters
They need our help
They need our support
Let's support them to regain their voices

They feel all eyes are on them
Not for good reasons but shame
Theirs is bedlam

Rape has eaten them
They need our support
Yes they need the voice
They need our voices

I see rapists
I see warlords
They all are agents
The agents of imperialists
I see them conspiring against innocent women
I see them as they rape girls and children
Please stop this madness
Those victims need their voices

I see greed for power
I see the world in disorder
I see double standards
Those with power in the hands
Are looking at their agendas
Even by sacrificing innocent women
Instead of giving them the voice

The victims of rape are suffering
They are but dead but living
How can we ease their sufferings?
How can we bring smiles on their faces?
Without giving their voices back?
They need their voices back

They are called all names
Wherever they go theirs has been shame
Some have them to blame

Some do even shun them
They see them as an abomination
Again, is it their burden?
Please give them the voices

I urge concerned and caring communities
All affected communities
Please create opportunities
Based on possible possibilities
Help the victims of rape and other brutalities
Just give them the lost voices
We need to face such realities
That the victims are still members of communities

I urge the international community
To create a modality
By which to address this calamity
Let's create possible conviviality
For the victims of rape
Let's give them the voice
Indeed they need the voice

We must address the trauma
It makes victims a misnomer
We need to seriously address this drama
Victims of rape face such difficult encounter
They've lost their karma
Let's do one important thing
Let us show understanding
Then give them their voices
The world needs to understand
We all need to stand with such victims

We needs to see their sarcasms
We need to close the chasms
That they face wherever they go
We need to support and help them
By just give them the voice
Given them another chance

Rape victims are always stigmatized
Yes, they are traumatized
Some communities shun them
They do that out of their ignorance
Others do bear with them
They do that out of their cognizance
They'd give them voice

I see victims with their lost radiance
They've lost their confidence
Long gone is their prominence
With all their innocence
They still bear the wrenches
They're the victims of rape violence
They lost their voices

I see victims with their patience
With exception indulgence
Despite all the negligence
They still soldier on with decency
If such victims are given voice
Slowly they'd go back to normalcy
However it is a process
It needs one to be courageous
I am sure with the new voice

Victims have many chances
To rebuild their lives
Especially if they are given voice

Some decided to forgive and move on
Though they can't forget what happened to them
There are those who were raped in front of their children
Others were raped in front of their parents
Others in front of their spouses
Their predators did that to kill their spirits
They broke the bond that bound them together
Victims end up in silence
After losing their voices

Some were raped and tortured
Others were left for dead
Others had their private parts destroyed
Many their bodies and souls were bruised
Many brutalities were committed
Not to mention indescribable barbarities committed
All these vices robbed the victims of their voices

Other victims were brutally murdered
Not to mention those who were maimed
They had their bodies deformed
Their beauties were destroyed
So, too, their spirits were dampened
They'll always be victims
That will cry for justice
As they hunt for their voices
Rape destroys many more than victims
Their relatives too become victims

They all nurse horrible pains
However with different degrees
Enormous is their stress
So, too they need a voice

Relatives of victims will always feel sad
Rape destroyed their world
Others will embark on revenges
Though revenge adds more damages
Revenge doesn't bring the voice back
The right thing is to get the voice back

Again, what can we do?
What should we do?
This is their plight
Yes a sealed predicament
Everybody has to understand it
Understanding will give victims the voices

Some societies take it too far
They condemn the victims of rape
They have no time to probe
They just judge blindly and conservatively
Instead of finding remedy
They end up becoming jeopardy
They victims suffer even more
Because their voice is no more
Under the honor killings they butcher them
Under archaic culture they shun them
They have nowhere to go
They live in a no go
Let's be the place for them to go

For, we can give them the voices

Instead of accusing warlords
And those who supply them weapons
Humans are accusing victims
Yes, they blindly and falsely accusing victims
Did they choose to?
Please give them voices

How many women are raped?
Yes, many are raped
In many unsafe streets
Many are raped in cities
Aren't they humans to deserve security?
Their voice is their security
So we need to give them voices

Where are the governments?
Where are law enforcement agents?
Where are the presidents
Where are rights activists
I want them hither
I want them to ponder
Let them ponder on this argument
Yes it is based on possibility
Suppose the victims were their daughters
Suppose they were their sweet mothers
Suppose the victims were their sisters
Will presidents maintain silence?
We'd like to hear their voices
As they make logical noises
Noises of giving women voices

For the victims of brutal and mindless killings
They are haplessly killed by fellow human beings
Should such killers be treated like human beings?
We need to stop such savageries
Such sacrilegious acts befit not human beings
We need to put them to an end urgently
Let's raise our voices

The world needs to know
However with sorrow
With indignation and horror
Sure, the world needs to know
That innocent humans are perishing
Greed and ignorance are decimating them
The world needs to stand with them
To make sure that such criminality is thwarted
Let's add our voices
Let's stop wars

There are innocent people in this world
That is wiped out with latitude
People with albinism are being felled
Just for megalomania and stupidity
The world needs solidarity
To see to it such innocent people are saved

Many unborn babies are killed
They're conceived almost every day in this world
Diabolical cultures are to blame
Freedom without responsibility is to blame
Young girls are being preyed on
And there are no laws to protect them

We need to give them voices

Innocent babies are dumped
Lucky ones are abandoned
The situation is alarming
Many are killed
Premature pregnancies are increasing
We need to do something
To save such innocent beings
It is only through giving them the voices
They'll be able to take on the vice

Rape has become a weapon of war
Those committing it think they are winning the war
Again, rape is the weapon of cowards
Rape is the weapon of criminals
Low-abiding people should not use this brutal weapon
What type of weapon is this?
That steals victims' voices

Look at how diabolic this crime is
Relatives are forced to rape their loved ones
Sacrilegious things happen
A real man can't use the barrel of gun to force others
Forcing them to commit things even animals can't do to others
Such a person is accidentally human

A real man does not rape
A real man does keep
Yes, a real man is a protector
A real man is conciliator

Why behaving like an ape
Rape is for chickens
Those committing rape are but chickens
Rapists should be made to pay for their crimes

Rapists should be forced to wear sacks
They'd be smeared with ash
Then they must receive some thwacks
Rapists should be put before the mass
So that they can be ashamed
This will send signals
To all criminals
Rape should not be tolerated
For it destroys communities
Rape destroys families
It has killed many souls

Long time in some African societies
Rapists had their balls crushed
Rapists were treated like leprosy
They received no clemency
Nobody felt for them indeed
Committing rape was person's death sentence
For those who were propitious
Ended up receiving heavy sentence

The Plight of Women

I know this will be an issue
That will attract censure
Some will have it to mock
It'll obviously cause a lot of pique
Again, isn't real and true?
That despite our advancement
Women all over the world are still exploited
Most of them have lost their voices

They are exploited based on gender
Sadly this has become a culture
In some societies women are treated like a property
That any person can claim to own
I know where women own women
They marry them and find men for them
Women are sadly used like equipment
Simply because of their gender
Anybody can detain their voices
And leave them without a voice

Turning women into chattels
Is but exploitation
They are many in huts and castles
Women are not chattels
We need to stop the *thingification* of women
They're as worth as men
We're all human beings
So making women things
In other words is making men things

Men and women depend on each other
So let's respect each other
We need to value each other
As we care for each other
So, we must all have a voice

Women are suffering
Indeed, they are suffering
They're suffering in the hands of their husbands
They are put in men's lineages
This is done without giving them the voice
If we don't practically stop this vice
Many will still suffer
For, they won't have their voices

Many are robbed of their voices
The *status quo* wants their compliance
We need to give back their voices
So that they can contribute to our fullness
Sexual discrimination is a menace
That the world needs to fight
We need to have an equal place
Before laws and before incomes
This is their voices

Some are well educated
Well qualified and nurtured
Yet they are exploited
They are objectified and owned
Look at how some are salaried
You'll wonder and shudder
Men are highly paid

Women are lowly paid
Is this happening in this century?
This will be your question
The answer is the voice
Women need their voices

Try to find the answer for it
Try to slink into their boot
I am sure you'll get it
As you ask if it were you
Try to imagine honestly
You'll get what many don't
We need gender equality
We need gender security
This is not a choice
It is a social onus
Give females their voices

Patriarchal system is to blame
Yes, it has created this crime
What a shame!
To rob females their voice
Isn't this a crime?
To silence women's voices
Tell me
What is its name?
The name of this crime

Females in many places can't walk free
They always are under fear
Yes, they're under fear of rape
They are under fear of sexual assault

87

They lost hope
Ask them if they enjoy security
Their answer will be a big nope

We need safe streets
Safe sidewalks and cities
We need safe countries
Same homes and families
Where women will feel safe
Where women will enjoy protection
Just like any member of the society
They must have a voice

In many countries females are second-class citizens
Yet they make a big chunk of populace
We need to erase this discrepancy
To see to it that females are treated equally
Why killing them for honour
Whose honour that doesn't belong to them
Why continuing with such victimizing honour
Honour is about equality and grandeur
Let's respect people as people but not based on gender

Some institutions treat women as half beings
They treat them like nonhuman beings
Some think they have no feelings
Some kill their feelings
They discriminate against them
Others torture them
Discrimination is evil
Those espousing it are evil
We need to fight such institutions

We need to shun these institutions
If possible we must criminalise them
Essentially, we must banish them
Let's raise our voices

In some societies women face genital mutilation
Others face beatings and humiliation
Time has come now for the world
To step in and put such practices to an end
We need all to understand
Women are as human as men
Let's give them their voice
Let's respect their place in the society
Let them live like any other member of the society
Yes, for, they have a voice

Some institutions allege to be godly
Ironically they actually act ungodly
Whoever that claims to be godly
Must treat people equally
Discrimination is ungodly
Exploitation is ungodly
If anything,
Such understanding is gory
Let's condemn them with our voices
Let's make noises showing our resistance

We need to bury discriminative cultures
Such cultures are but our societal ulcers
We need to bring changes
Yes, we need urgent changes
We need to treat such cultures like garbage

For we all know their damages
Their dwellings should be in historical wastebaskets
Anti-female cultures must become things of the past
They must be completely uprooted
Laws must be purposely and urgently enacted
To see to it that sexual discrimination is outlawed

Sexual discrimination is archaic
It is ridiculously inimical
It is outdated and tyrannical
So stopping it is not the matter of choice
Fighting against is our onus
Nobody should stop us
From giving women their voice
They need it back and at once
For it is naturally theirs

Some cultures force women into forced marriage
Forced marriage is but carnage
Why'd men force women into forced marriage?
Are they the ones supposed to get married by those they
choose?
Aren't such victims unable to make decisions that are sound?
Forcing girls into forced marriage is a crime
Those committing it must be punished
Women have their voices
They must be left to make their choices

Those who resist forced marriages
End up being brutally murdered
They pretext given is honour killings
Can killing be an honourable thing?

The honor that depends on killings
Is indeed not honour
It is but mere horror

Some say a man is a head
And a woman is a body
Is there any creature that can live without a head?
Where will its brains be
Where will its power of reasoning be?
Being a torso is lucking sense of reasoning
And being headless
Is being reasonless
Are women real reasonless?
Don't they have brains and self-consciousness?
Women, just like men, are born with voices

I know many women
They are tied to man's bad omen
They suffer in the hands of men
Simply because they are women
Being a woman is not a sin
Being a man should never cause a din
What I know we're all humans
Yes, we're all equal humans
We all were born with our voices

To discriminate against women is inhuman
Even to question their intellect is inhuman
We just have the same acumen
We face the same challenges
There might be slight differences
All depends on how one looks at the situation

Our difference is but a social construction
That needs true deconstruction
Yes, we need to deconstruct all evil notions

Look at that rural woman
I see her going to the farm
I can see the baby on her back
I see a hoe on her shoulder
She weeds and works on the farm
Again, before time
She's another assignment to do
She will collect firewood
Look at her on her way back
The baby on the back
The hoe on her shoulder
Yet still, the firewood on her head
She has lost her voice
She needs her voice back

What does her husband carry?
Only his hoe
Does he care or worry
That his wife is overdone?
Why should he worry?
His wife is like his many oxen
Whatever must be done?
The wife has to do it
For she's no voice
Yes, she's no choice

As they arrive back home all tired
The wife won't rest
She'll hit the road
She'll go to the well
Water at home is needed
Once again her baby on her back
Her pot on her head
The husband will rest
Or just go the neighbourhood
Another will turn on the radio
As he waits for food

Back home the wife'll return
Cooking will begin
Yet the baby will scream
It will need her attention
Even if her hubby is at home
He'll never bother to attend the honey
He'll read a newspaper
Or just have a nap
Once all is done
The wife will prepare the table
Then, she'll humbly call him to join the table

Once eating is done
Dishes are there waiting for her
The husband will be done
He'll choose where to go
He decides to have a shuteye again
His job is done
The wife's job has begun
She has to wash the dishes

As dishes are done
Evening is approaching
She goes back to the cooking
Out the husband is going
He wants to link up with friends
He needs to hear their stories
He'll kill time with friends

Thereafter he goes back home
As he arrives back home
He demands for hot water
Yes, hot water to take a shower
The wife will have already boiled the water
She'll pick up the bucket and take it to the restroom
She will rush back to the bedroom
To attend a crying one
Her cooking is there staring at her
It needs water refilling
She will jump and rush to the kitchen
Where the goat is too attacking her cooking

As if this isn't enough
The big man will bellow
"What's wrong with you woman?"
He will holler again
"Woman where are you?
"Bring me my other shirt"
"This one is dirty"

The wife will abandon what she's doing
She'll rush again in the bedroom
She'll pick up and take a clean shirt

To the husband who is waiting
She'll go back to the bedroom
Where the baby is crying
She'll pick the baby and heard to the kitchen
To go on with cooking

As the night falls
Her works are still going on
Her body is aching
She hasn't had a recreation
She will pick up the washbasin
And start showering the young one
Suddenly others are arriving
They have been to school
They'll come with their demands

They'll all need food
They'll need shower too
On her feet the wife will jump
With her soft voice she'll hum
She will go to the washroom
She has a washbasin to pick up
She'll fill it up with water
She still will be a supervisor
To see all children get a shower
After all children get their shower
She'll send them to their bedrooms

Her ordeal is not done
She'll have other chores to have done
Patiently she will keep waiting
For bedtime to come

The husband has come back home
He's still energetically calm
After his shower is done
He'll head to the bedroom
As he waits for her to come
He's waiting for time to come
When all children are benumbed
The wife'll go to her bedroom to make a bed
Then she'll go back to the kitchen
She'll make sure everything is fine
Then she will round up her routine
After making sure that everything is fine
She will check if all doors are locked
Off she goes to bed!

After all chores out of bedroom are done
An exhausted wife will complain
"What a tough this day has been"
She will deposit the baby in its crib
Then jump in bed close to her hubby
In the bed she will breakdown
Her husband's been waiting
To her direction he'll turn
As he wants the "thing"
The wife will complain
She will say "I'm tired"
The husband will retort
"Don't you know this is a marriage right?"
The game will start
He'll go two or three *jaunts*
After getting what he wants
You'll hear him as he snorts

The new day kicks in
The ordeal repeats again
With all of her yesterday pain
The wife becomes an early bird
She wakes up before everybody
She prepares children for school
Then she picks her baby and her tool
Off she goes to the farm
Despite doing all such wonderful things
Some husbands still beat their wives
Despite giving them all such rewards
Some husbands never thanked their wives!

Look at this city wife
She still has her strife
She indeed still a wife
She is the wife of the same brand of man
A man who is above a woman
Whose voice's above that of a woman

Like her husband she's employed
However she has more on her plate
As early in the morning they wake
They prepare themselves for work
The wife does a lot of work
While the husband just listen to news

Remember
They have a few children to look after
The schooling children of course
Mother will take care of them
She'll prepare them
97

She'll prepare breakfast for them
As she sees them go
She turns to herself

Indeed
Her husband is ready
He's waiting for her to leave
She hurriedly prepares herself
Off they leave for workplaces!
If they work in the same office
Lucky them
If they work in different places and offices
Everybody will take her or his town bus
If they are blessed to have a car
A hubby will drop her

As their works are done
The hubby will come for her
He'll come and collect her
As they rush to go home
Their children are back home
As they wait for them
The couple will arrive home
After making sure that everything is in order
The hubby will want to go the bar
He has friends to chat with
They have the business to deal with
The wife will be left at home to attend the children

The move will start her chores
While the hubby is doing the talking
The wife is at home doing the cooking

So, too, she is doing the washing
She'll iron her hubby's clothes her children' and hers
She'll go through children' assignments
As she listens to their complaints
If she'd time she'll watch a soap opera
If time is not on her side
She'll put the soap opera aside
She'll do all chores
As she waits for her husband to come back home

After getting a couple of beers
The man will retire back home
When he left he was calm
After swallowing some beers
His sanity is now history
He becomes a provocateur
He is talking about his degrees
And how harder he worked for his thesis
He talks nonstop
He's now on the top
His wife is used to him
So, she doesn't bother with him

He too knows his wife
He doesn't want to stir strife
He heads for the bedroom
He has *high steam*
He waits for the time to come
He badly needs his *yum*
Here the wife has come
He welcomes her in the bedroom
The wife has never been in a hurry

She starts her night with the preliminary
She has notice it in his expression
He seems to wait for something

Knowing the lioness she is
He just lays down waiting
He is good at timing
The wife at a snail's pace
She seems to careless
The hubby keeps his peace
Patience is the mother of success

As the hubby silently curses
The wife doesn't mind
She goes on with night exercise
She perfects her rituals
Once she's sure everything's precise
She methodically jumps on the bed

As the wife lands in bed
The husband has no fortitude
Proposes the husband
"Honey, turn this side"
The wife doesn't yield
She simply does respond
"Children are still roused?
How long will it take for them to be at it?
Please don't ask about it
I don't want to cross the line

I thus have to close the line
Enough is enough
You know what follows

People with Albinism

I learnt the plight of people with albinism with shock
I didn't know that these people are becoming extinct
I used to hear extinction on animals and assets
For human being such phenomenon is totally shocker

In the first instance I could not believe
The news truly and badly numbed my nerves
Given that this crime is obvious
It is time the all of us
To stand and say never
Let's say never to this criminality
Everybody say never to this brutality
Let's raise our voices
So that victims can have a voice

When it came to my knowledge that human are felled
I am told wrong beliefs are to blame
It took me a very long time
To believe that human could commit such sacrilege
Where do they get the courage?
To turn their fellows into items
There must be a loophole
The authorities have to blame
They need to give the voice

The media has it all
It is all over the world
Some countries in African are implicated
People with albinism are felled

They're killed like animals
Like elephants and rhinos
Even animals are far better
For they are protected
Yes, animals have voices
Powers that be have given them the voice

I hear many conferences and campaigns
They are about preserving endangered animals
What of people with albinism?
Aren't they endangered organisms?
People of albinism are killed for their body parts!
Aren't they dying in silence?
Why then shouldn't we give them voice?

Wrong beliefs are to blame
Ignorance, greed and corruption are to blame
Complicity and laxity by the authorities are to blame
Why humans should be hunted like animals
Why do we protect extinct animals?
Yet we fail to protect our sisters and brothers
Yes, we are letting down the people with albinism
We need to give them the voice

I saw graphic pictures of the victims
Many are maimed carelessly
Others are killed mercilessly
Others are exhumed
All is done in the name of wealth
Can wealth be gotten without hard work?
What type of wealth this is
Isn't this madness

I call upon affected countries
I call upon all authorities in these countries
They must fulfil their sacred duties
Of which is to preserve human lives
Don't turn humans into animals
This is a sin-cum-crime

People with albinism are people like others
They deserve all rights just like others
Being born with albinism and other disorders
Should not be turned into a death sentence
We need to enact tough laws to combat this
To see to it that people with albinism are safe
Yes, they must have their own voices

They deserve to live like any other persons
They are the citizens of their countries like other citizens
So they'd be treated like any other citizens
Their rights must be protected
Their security must be guaranteed
For they are humans just like any other persons
They were born with their voices

The numbers of the victims are alarming
We need to do something
Education is an important thing
For such criminals killing other human beings
Fighting corruption is another thing
For it encourages greed for wealth
Countries should fight corruption
Let's raise our voices against it

Lt's declare such killings an international menace
Let's join hands to curb this violence
We need to stand together with firmness
Let's show our stance against this malevolence
Violence is violence
No way can it secure any tolerance
We need to take on it without any mercy
Yes, let us take on it mercilessly
We need to raise our voices
For the victims have long lost their voices

END

Printed in the United States
By Bookmasters